Hidden Treasure Keys
In Broken Vessels

Copyright © 2019 by **Kimberly Fields Whitfield.**

All rights reserved. No part of this publication may be reproduced, stored in a retrieval system, or transmitted in any form by any means, electronically, mechanical, photocopying, recording or otherwise without written permission of the copyright owner.

ISBN-13: 978-1-948605-08-3

I Still Love Him Devotional

By: Kimberly Fields Whitfield

DEDICATION

This devotional journal was inspired from my Amazing Journey and in memory of my late husband Marion "Whit" Whitfield. This journal is dedicated to our Treasures, all our children: Nell, Chelle, Sherell, Karrington, Veronica, Kell, and Khayla. My dearly beloved treasures, always remember you are valued and loved and I want you to never forget the inspired Words of Jesus in John 16:33:

"These things I have spoken unto you, that in me ye might have peace. In the world, ye shall have tribulations: but be of good cheer; I have overcome the world."

About Kimberly Fields Whitfield

Kim began writing for her grandmother's great-great Aunt Lina who was approximately 108 years old. Kim has always enjoyed journaling life's events and accomplishments, cooking and being creative. She is also known as Kreative Blessings because she enjoys adding a certain uniqueness or flare to her recipes when cooking, when she styles hair, decorating, teaching a class or workshop.

Kim is the daughter of the King, born out of wedlock and in a housing project. She has always desired to be happily married with a large family, educated and a prosperous career. Even after having two children and her first marriage failed, the desire became even stronger to build to happy family. After a matter of a few short months of being divorced, Kim was married to the love of her life, Marion "Whit" Whitfield for nearly 25 years.

Kim is a first-generation college student. Although the road to graduation had many curves and turns. She initially started at a four-year HBCU and dropped out resorting to getting an Associate Business Degree and completing a Master Cosmetology Program at a technical college. Afterwards, Kim obtained her license to own and operate her first business which was Design Studios #1 Hair Gallery in Waynesboro, GA. When happiness prevailed, her husband Whit encouraged her to go back to school. Kim immediately started attending another four-year HBCU while operating in her beauty salon.

At only twenty-five years old, Kim had a lot on her plate as she dealt with a blended family because Whit had also been previously married with four daughters. After getting her momentum back, Kim completed her business degree and even continued to earn a dual graduate degree. She received a Bachelor's of Science Business Degree and even continued to earn a dual graduate Master's of Science and Management (MSM) and Business Administration (MBA).

She has had a few business ventures to include owning and operating her own salon for almost 30 years, a couple restaurants and a catering service, as well as pursued an alternative route to teaching in the public-school system.

Kim enjoys cooking, traveling, having fun, entertaining her family and friends and soaring high to reaching her dreams. Just when she was at a peak enjoying life with Whit, a storm came raging. Whit lost his battle to Prostate cancer in the prime of their lives.

Kim has since dedicated her life to the Mission field of helping others as she launched The W.H.I.T. Project Foundation to honor her husband's legacy.

(Www.whitprojectfoundation.com)

About The Devotional

This 52-day devotional was developed during a period in my life when my days seemed most dark. Cancer is anything that disrupts or attempts to disrupt a family.

Families who need to gain strength while experiencing anything that interrupts your everyday lifestyle such as imprisonment, financial crisis or death can benefit from this devotional. Find your happy place! That place for Whit was hearing Kynsley call him "PaPa." He often shared with others how this little girl was his therapy and how they had a special connection.

Whit often bragged on Kynsley having an old soul, and how much she brightened his day giving him more joy in the run of a day than any radiation or chemotherapy could.

Whit and I meditated daily on Psalm 91, but we studied many scriptures taking our relationship with God to another level.

Isaiah 45:3 has been my soul guiding scripture while launching the W.H.I.T. Project foundation alongside writing this devotional.

It is my hope that whatever trial you are experiencing that you will use this devotional time to journal to discover the keys of **love, faith, trust, hope, peace, compassion,** and **grace** which are the hidden treasures to unlock the gateway to enjoying your amazing journey.

Throughout this book, you will find seven questions and task pertaining to the acronym of our names as God gave me:

W.H.I.T.K.I.M. Daily Coping Mechanism:

What & How I Think

Keep Inspiring & Motivating Others

1) What HIDDEN thoughts come to mind from reading and digging deeper into the scriptures, and what can you TREASURE and be thankful for from them?

2) How has God helped you, a BROKEN VESSEL, cope with your current situation and improve your days?

3) Is there anything else, or another BROKEN area in your life, or something or someone dear to you, that you need God to move in, fix or make better?

4) Think about taking time for yourself and helping others because it builds relationships that can be TREASURED. It may seem difficult to do at this time, but it can be soothing as it heals your baffled

mind. Your thinking is changing now, so set some goals this week you can TREASURE forever. Can you make a list of simple ways to help yourself and others?

5) Keep a list of acts of kindness shown to you this week, and show some sort of gratitude, either by calls, cards, text or email.

6) Inspire someone you appreciate today, to let them know what they are doing is worthy. Perhaps a nurse, therapist, clerk, custodian, teacher, coworker, church member, family, friend and Etc.

7) Motivate and encourage someone who may be having a bad day, week or is in a bad situation.

KEYS TABLE OF CONTENT

About Kimberly Fields Whitfield v

About The Devotional viii

Key 1: Love ....
    Pieces Of Me It Must Be Love 1

Key 2: Faith ....
    Super Charged Ain't No Stopping Us Now 16

Key 3: Trust ....
    I'm Blessed Let's Do It Again 31

Key 4: Hope ....
    Happy People Choosing Hope 46

Key 5: Joy ....
    Game Changer Sexual Healing And Sex Therapy 61

Key 6: Peace ....
    It's A Love Thang All The Way 76

Key 7: Compassion ....
    Back Down Memory Lane I Can't Stop Loving Him 91

Key 8: Grace ....
    He Promised Me Love And Happiness 106

Memories 118

Introducing
Days 1-7
Love
Pieces Of Me
It Must Be Love

DAY 1

(KJV) Psalm 23:1 **The Lord is my shepherd; I shall not want.**

This is a beautiful scriptural text and I'm particularly excited to be starting with this text. I knew Jesus at an early age. Although I may always not have been in the best relationship with him, he has always been with me. It has been proven that he has always been with me.

Several times, when the Lord wanted to remind me about his unending love – The Lord is my shepherd overwhelms my thoughts.

Finances can come up really short when you are caring for a loved one or going through a struggle. Time is money, and caregiving may not always allow time for you to work through everything - job, family, caregiving etc. But two important clauses stayed with me: "The Lord is my shepherd", "I shall not want", one being a function of the other. I shall not want because the Lord is my Shepherd.

What *hidden* thoughts come to mind from reading and digging deeper into the scriptures, and what can you *treasure* and be thankful for from them?

DAY 2

(ESV) Matthew 6:33 **But seek first the kingdom of God and his righteousness, and all these things will be added to you.**

What does it mean to seek? After continuously seeking doctor after doctor, and coming up with the diagnoses, Whit and I learned to seek God and allow him to give us strength to endure everything else to come. We learned that only God could give us step by step directions.

Also, I remember misplacing Whit's prescription one morning. I woke up with a headache, I was barely organized the night before, worn out from taking care of him. He had just been diagnosed with lymphoma; cancer found in the eye. I had gotten some drugs, but I needed to get others. However, unfortunately I misplaced the tiny prescription paper. I had to 'seek' it out.

Remember when Jesus said the kingdom of heaven is like a woman seeking for a pearl? The seeking takes place in our hearts. We seek out God's kingdom in our hearts just as Whit and I had to seek to find the right doctors, the right treatments and the right step by step coping mechanisms to help endure the process.

How has God helped you, a broken vessel, cope with your current situation and improve your days?

_____
_____
_____
_____
_____
_____
_____
_____
_____
_____
_____
_____
_____
_____
_____
_____
_____
_____
_____

DAY 3

(KJV) Proverb 3:5-6 **Trust in the Lord with all thine heart; and lean not unto thine own understanding. In all thy ways acknowledge him, and he shall direct thy path.**

Trust is an important ingredient in every relationship, even our relationship with God! My marriage was strengthened through trust. Love is important, very important but trust takes the relationship farther than love will, even when one of you has been diagnosed with prostate cancer or maybe experiencing another terrifying situation. I didn't just trust Whit as my partner, we also trusted God in our relationship. People don't divorce because there's no love, many times it's because there's no trust!

Is there anything else, or another broken area in your life, or something or someone dear to you, that you are trusting God to move in, fix or make better?

_____
_____
_____
_____
_____
_____
_____
_____
_____
_____
_____
_____
_____
_____
_____
_____
_____
_____
_____
_____

DAY 4

(NKJV) 3 **The Lord says, Call to Me, and I will answer you, and show you great and mighty things, which you do not know.'**

"…which you do not know." Walking with God starts with taking baby steps. I had no idea how much I was going to survive when Whit's sickness first started. I almost reached my breaking point a day prior to speaking to a friend in my time of need. She stated: "My sister, you have endured much but God's strength is amazing through you and that is the only reason you are still standing strong." The Lord is always listening and ready to help in our time of need.

Think about taking time for yourself and helping others because it builds relationships that can be *treasured*. It may seem difficult to do at this particular time, but it can be soothing as it heals your baffled mind. Your thinking is changing now, so set some goals this week you can *treasure* forever. Can you make a list of simple ways to help yourself and others?

_____
_____
_____
_____
_____
_____
_____
_____
_____
_____
_____
_____

DAY 5

(KJV) 2 Corinthians 5:7 **For we walk by faith, not by sight.**

(MSG) 2 Co 5:7 **Its what we trust in but don't yet see that keeps us going.**

Over the past days, we not only discussed the importance of love, but also how trust is a secret ingredient in every relationship, more so, in our relationship with God. Jesus is called the Good Shepherd (see John 10: 11, 14) and his sheep know his voice and follow him. A shepherd is simply someone who tends and rears sheep but can also mean someone who guides or directs in a particular way. To follow him, we will learn to do by faith– what we don't yet see that keeps us going– and not by what we see.

We may not always see our future outcome in any given situation, but our faith in God is what keeps us going knowing that he has prepared the way.

Keep the faith! Keep a list of acts of kindness shown to you this week, and show some sort of gratitude, either by calls, cards, text or email.

DAY 6

(KJV) Psalm 119:105 **Thy word is a lamp unto my feet, and a light unto my path.**

Thanksgiving has always been my favorite Holiday. In past years, I would invite our family and enjoy the Thanksgiving Holiday. However, the year 2008 presented many dark moments. Whit's biopsy revealed that he had cancer a week before Thanksgiving.

Earlier that year, in March, my daughter quit college and then on July 5th, my son committed a crime and went to prison. If there was any time, I needed light more, I needed light through those dark times that year. One may not know what the outcome will be. What's the outcome of prostate cancer? What is the likely outcome of being a dropout? Is prison not worse?

However, I stayed with God's word, and like walking through a dark path, it was a lamp for me through 2008.

Inspire someone you appreciate today, to let them know what they are doing is worthy, and that they have been a light to your dark path. Perhaps a nurse, therapist, clerk, custodian, teacher, coworker, church member, family, friend and Etc.

_____
_____
_____
_____
_____
_____
_____
_____
_____
_____
_____
_____
_____
_____
_____
_____

DAY 7

(NKJV) Luke 17:6 **"faith as a mustard seed, you can say to this mulberry tree, 'Be pulled up by the roots and planted in the sea,' and it obeys you."**

We already saw how Faith (what we do not see) contrasts with sight (what we see). Faith is hope that we will have our desires and it is that hope that helps us pursue it. Seeing a mountain (the problem) will not help us move, instead it will leave us stagnant, in fear and in doubt. And this is the opposite of faith. Faith isn't blind doggedness, it is seeing the problem from where God sees it!

Motivate and encourage someone who may be having a bad day, week or is in a bad situation.

Introducing
Days 8-14
Faith
Super Charged
Ain't No Stopping Us Now

DAY 8

(ESV) Ephesians 2:8 **For by grace you have been saved through faith. And this is not your own doing; it is the gift of God.**

Salvation is God's gift. A gift means you didn't work for it – it is a function of the benevolence of the giver. No matter what one is going through, for some it is fighting cancer, others poverty, bankruptcies, loved ones imprisoned, pregnancy, job loss, and even death of loved ones, salvation becomes a way of escape. These are moments it feels as though one is losing it, but when we call on Him, he will save us and comfort us.

What *hidden* thoughts come to mind from reading and digging deeper into the scripture, and what can you *treasure* or be thankful for from it?

DAY 9

(BBE) Joshua 1:9 **"Take heart and be strong; have no fear and do not be troubled; for the Lord your God is with you wherever you go."**

On Sunday October 29, 2017, Whit's father died. On the Monday following Whit's dad's death, Whit and I was able to plan and finalize the entire funeral arrangement. Whit had a terrible fall a day prior to the funeral, which was also one of our daughter's birthday Friday November 3, 2017.

Once Whit fell, he was rushed to the hospital. He was placed in ICU and could not attend his father's funeral the next day due to the acute complications. He broke a couple of ribs which punctured his lungs and cracked his neck. I felt stretched out because I had so many duties and responsibilities: motherhood, wife, elementary school teacher and a church leader on the state and local level. Among all of these challenges, my husband was still being treated for stage four cancer.

It was not until February 8, 2018 Whit transitioned. I hope to tell all the people I meet that cancer did not take him out; it was the terrible fall. My, my, my; What a crisis! There are no soothing words like "Take heart and be strong; have no fear and do not be troubled; for the Lord your God is with you wherever you go." Even after a terrible fall!

How has God helped you, a *broken vessel*, cope with your current situation or another terrible problem?

DAY 10

(NKJV) Philippians 4:13 **I can do all things through Christ who strengthens me.**

I gained strength from hurtful situations. "The strength helped me get through my husband's death.

Through Whit's period of sickness, I had eleven months preparation not realizing that I was actually being strengthened in preparation for Whit's transitioning.

Everyday writing helped me to get through the storm –I wrote daily, either to document how I felt, what I was going through, God's promise to me… I simply wrote anything I felt I should. Somehow, I knew my story will one day encourage somebody somewhere.

And in all these things, our testimony will always be: "I can do all things through Christ who strengthens me."

Is there anything else, or another *broken* area in your life, or something or someone dear to you, that you need God to move in, fix or make better?

_____
_____
_____
_____
_____
_____
_____
_____
_____
_____
_____
_____
_____
_____
_____
_____

DAY 11

(MSG) Philippians 4:13 **Whatever I have, wherever I am, I can make it through anything in Christ who made me who I am.**

In the darkest moments, when it feels like walls are caving in on us, we will still have two gifts and can make it out strong. It's the WHAT and the WHERE. There will always be what you have and where you are. What has God given you? Where has he placed you? If he has blessed your union with children and grandchildren and even if you have lost your husband like I did, God has still given you family. Family is a gift.

Think about taking time for yourself and helping others because it builds relationships that can be *treasured*. It may seem difficult to do at this particular time, but it can be soothing as it heals your baffled mind. Your thinking is changing now, so set some goals and take a lot of pictures this week that you can *treasure* forever. Can you make a list of simple ways to help yourself and others?

_____
_____
_____
_____
_____
_____
_____
_____
_____
_____
_____
_____

DAY 12

(NKJV) Jeremiah 29:11 **For I know the thoughts that I think toward you, says the Lord, thoughts of peace and not of evil, to give you a future and a hope.**

The place of trust in our relationship with God cannot be overstretched. Many times, we want to go in our own strength and end up hurting ourselves. Many times, God's understanding is as simple as a small man like David going all out with a sling and five stones, against a giant like a stroke or cancer.

We have to go deeper in God's word for our endurance. It could be overwhelming and force us to do one of two things: break us down to the point we stop living or keep us moving forward standing on God's promises to give us a future and a hope.

We were not glad Whit had a stroke, but without him having one, we would not have known that the cancer was on the rise… This was our giant and it was time for us to declare war digging deeper into God's word fighting our fears while focusing on the promises we had vowed to stay true to one another until death due us part.

Keep a list of acts of kindness shown to you this week, and show some sort of gratitude, either by calls, cards, text or email.

_____
_____
_____
_____
_____
_____
_____
_____
_____
_____
_____
_____
_____
_____
_____
_____
_____
_____
_____

DAY 13

(NIV) Matthew 6:34 **Don't worry about tomorrow, for tomorrow will worry about itself. Each day has enough trouble of its own.**

Worry is such a terrible thing I had to fight through Whit's sickness. Many times, I wanted to get into worrying and feeling sorry for myself, but that's when I am weakest. I draw strength from pushing away worry and embracing what God has said about tomorrow. Even when it was obvious that Whit was going to transition after his complications. I kept saying to myself that God holds my tomorrow, I have nothing to fear.

Inspire someone you appreciate today, to let them know what they are doing is worthy. Perhaps a nurse, therapist, clerk, custodian, teacher, coworker, church member, family, friend etc.

DAY 14

(NKJV) Psalm 23: 4 **Yea, though I walk through the valley of the shadow of death, I will fear no evil; You are with me.**

God was with me, has always been with me and is still with me. Whit said he was ready to go home a day before he transitioned. All that day he looked strong and kept telling me how much he loved me. I felt he was getting better. Whit was getting better to meet Jesus. The next day at 7pm he transitioned. He transitioned so peacefully.

I was supposed to be gripped by fear and overwhelmed by grief, but no, though I walk through the valley of the shadow of death, I feared no evil; God was there with me. I knew that God was there giving me strength and understanding as I watched Whit sleep so peacefully.

Motivate and encourage someone who may be having a bad day, week or is in a bad situation.

INTRODUCING
DAYS 15-21
TRUST
I'M BLESSED
LET'S DO IT AGAIN

DAY 15

(Isaiah 40:31) **They that wait on the Lord shall renew their strength; mount up with wings as eagles; run, and not be weary; walk and not faint!**

Waiting upon the Lord here is not passive, it is actually taking an action and when you take an action, others will see it and make remarks. "Your strength was amazing" a doctor complimented me on being strong and holding myself together. Again, this was another place where I had almost reached my breaking point. Instead, I declared and always stated to others that God's strength is amazing.

I endured so much. While it was important to have others encourage you, it was most important at that time for me to encourage myself and waiting and knowing that waiting on the Lord will strengthen me no matter what the challenges were. I had surmounted like an eagle and could not faint!

What *hidden* thoughts come to mind from reading and digging deeper into the scriptures, and what can you *treasure* and be thankful for from them?

DAY 16

(KJV) 2 Chronicles 7:14 **If my people, which are called by my name, shall humble themselves, and pray, and seek my face, and turn from their wicked ways; then will I hear from heaven, and will forgive their sin, and will heal their land.**

(BBE) 2 Chronicles 7:14 If my people, on whom my name is named, make themselves low and come to me in prayer, searching for me and turning from their evil ways; then I will give ear from heaven, overlooking their sin, and will give life again to their land.

An active way to wait on the Lord is to pray; our scripture says "if my people, on whom my name is named, make themselves low and come to me in prayer..." What's the prayer? Search for me, turn from evil ways... God says I will give ear from heaven, overlooking their sin, and will give life again to their land.

God is always ready to listen to us. We were the ones, TEAM WHIT STRONG made up of our family, friends, prayer partners and supporters to wait, to pray, to search and when we searched, we surely found comfort and strength just as Matthew 7:7 states: "Ask and it will be given to you; seek and you will find; knock and the door will be opened to you.

How has God helped you, a *broken vessel*, cope with your current situation and improve your days?

DAY 17

(NIV) Romans 8:28 **In All things God works for the good of those who love him and are called according to his purpose.**

"In all things…" We will see God working for the good of those who love him in all situations. Finances become draining when you are caring for someone who is ill. I dealt with the stress of paperwork through the period Whit transitioned. I could not believe that I still had to prove that I was the wife to certain organizations while closing out my husband's affairs —he died at 57. We were married for nearly 25 years. The stress of family, I was grieving, but in all of it God works for our good.

Is there anything else, or another *broken* area in your life, or something or someone dear to you, that you need God to move in, fix or make better?

DAY 18

(NIV) Galatians 6:9 **Let us not become weary in doing good, for at the proper time we will reap a harvest if we do not give up.**

It's quite difficult to see that someone else is hungry when you are starving, lacking resources or finances. It is difficult to see who is hurting when you are going through pains. When you have your hands full with a loved one coming down with cancer, it is quite difficult to see what anybody else is going through. At a time when Whit had a stroke, I was catering the first lady's tea party at our church. Whit encouraged me to stay and fulfill my obligation and have our youngest daughter Khayla take him to the VA hospital. Whit was not selfish. Rather than sit with him and look after him, my husband wanted me to help and serve others instead.

Whit reminded me that I could not do anything for him at that time. Only the doctors and the Master could help him. Again, I thank God that he had a stroke because it made us aware that his cancer returned. Whit encouraged me to keep serving, do good to others and that I will be rewarded.

Think about taking time for yourself and helping others because it builds relationships that can be treasured. It may seem difficult to do at this particular time, but it can be soothing as it heals your baffled mind. Your thinking is changing now, so set some goals this week you can treasure forever. Can you make a list of simple ways to help yourself and others?

_____
_____
_____
_____
_____
_____
_____
_____
_____
_____
_____
_____

DAY 19

(NIV) Philippians 1:6 **Be confident! He who began a good work in you will carry it to completion until the day of Christ Jesus.**

Be confident! Wait a second… he is not asking you to be confident in yourself, but that he who began a good work in you will carry it to completion until the day of Christ Jesus. That means the confidence is not in yourself – because as humans we have difficult times and weaknesses, we cannot lean on our own understanding –but rather our confidence is in He who began His good work in us, no matter what we face, he will carry it to completion!

Keep a list of acts of kindness shown to you this week, and show some sort of gratitude, either by calls, cards, text or email.

_____
_____
_____
_____
_____
_____
_____
_____
_____
_____
_____
_____
_____
_____
_____
_____
_____
_____

DAY 20

(KJV) Psalm 100:5 **For the Lord is good; his mercy is everlasting; and his truth endureth to all generations.**

The Lord is good, his mercy is everlasting: everlasting means "never ending." His mercy is never ending. That should gladden one's heart no matter the challenge. We know that God is good in the fact that His love will never end.

His truth endures through generations: God's truth does not change. His truth endures -retains its potency as truth - from one generation to another. Yes, he can be relied on, His truth, like his mercy will never change.

God called my dearly beloved, Whit home and two weeks later which was a week before our 25th wedding anniversary, another granddaughter was born. The WHIT Strong has blossomed even more because since that time, we have welcomed another granddaughter.

Inspire someone you appreciate today, to let them know what they are doing is worthy. Perhaps a nurse, therapist, clerk, custodian, teacher, coworker, church member, family, friend and etc.

DAY 21

(KJV) James 1:2-3 **Count it all joy when your faith is tested; (BBE) 3 Know the testing of your faith, gives the power of going on in hope.**

During the time that my husband battled with cancer, I had to battle with cancer. We all had to fight cancer; TEAM WHIT STRONG. It was not just Whit that was fighting cancer, we were both at war with the enemy who attempted to interrupt our family. This season was a time our faith was tried. James admonishes us and I encourage as many of you who are going through this battle as well, that you count your joy, when storms of life are raging.

Why? Every useful broken vessel goes through a testing stage to ascertain its usefulness and purpose. All human beings go through a period of test in institutions of learning, this determines if they are moving to the next stage or not. My husband's characteristics demonstrated to me that his purpose was fulfilled and that he was moving to the next level.

Motivate and encourage someone who may be having a bad day, week or is in a bad situation.

Introducing
Days 22-28
Hope
Happy People Choosing Hope

DAY 22

(KJV) Matthew 5:16 **Let your light shine before men, so they see your good works, and glorify your Father which is in heaven.**

I discovered I have a light. I am a chosen vessel, and I must not bury it but allow my light to shine and help other people see as well to strengthen as many people helping them avoid the ditches I encountered.

Over the years, I have been collecting messages and now I am sharing with others. Whit was sick for eleven months, so I started journaling. I started posting on social media to prevent answering everyone individually; I decided to let everyone know collectively. As I started to post, people began to respond, and many said that it was helping so many people. Several people informed me that they were going through similar situations and would share their stories as well.

This was a simple way of letting my light shine to help others.

Whhat *hidden* thoughts come to mind from reading and digging deeper into the scriptures, and what can you *treasure* and be thankful for from them?

DAY 23

(NKJV) Proverbs 30:5 **Every word of God is pure; He is a shield to those who put their trust in Him.**

In this devotional, we have laid a foundation of trusting God in our relationship with Him. Trust is needed for a family member or individuals going through what I went through with Whit.

In order to conquer, you will need all the trust in God you can have. Why trust him? The answer is in our hands-on manual which is our Bible! The Bible is made up of the Word of God spoken by the Holy Spirit. Then He will be able to shield us...shield us from hurt, from fear, and from giving up hope! Trust is how we invite Christ into our hearts and our lives.

How has God helped you, a *broken vessel*, cope with your current situation and improve your days?

DAY 24

(ESV) Galatians 5:22-23 **The fruit of the Spirit is love, joy, peace, patience, kindness, goodness, faithfulness, gentleness, self-control.**

Our manual says the 'fruit' of the Spirit 'is'... And then it goes ahead to highlight nine. One would have thought "the fruits of the Spirit are..." But it wasn't an error in writing. See it like a tree in your garden that has nine different kinds of fruits on it. If the tree is in your garden, then you can have access to different kinds of fruit on the tree. This reminds me of our relaxing journey touring the beautiful garden at the Biltmore Estate in Asheville, North Carolina. We were so mesmerized, or shall I say excited about God's creation. Whit and I got lost in the garden. We had to practice each of the fruits of the Spirit to keep our focus and get back on track. Our *love* for one another had us at *peace* although we were lost to find the *joy* by being *patient*, *kind* and *good* to each other while we *gently* held hands as we *controlled ourselves* of being fearful but walking in *faith* that God would see us through to a familiar place or back to our starting point.

Every child of God has access to His Spirit, in fact this is what makes us His children. This is a good way to practice faith and starve our fears in any bad situation.

Is there anything else, or another *broken* area in your life, or something or someone dear to you, that you need God to move in, fix or make better?

DAY 25

(ESV) Psalm 119:41 **Let your steadfast love come to me, O Lord, your salvation according to your promise.**

God's promise of salvation throughout the Old Testament is a major theme and David referred to it multiple times in his Psalm. David was a man after God's own heart. Salvation came to all in the person of Christ Jesus.

When you need salvation— that means you need a higher power to step in where you cannot do anything to help yourself. Many times, there is nothing one can do about imprisonment, poverty or cancer. It just seems as though one is submerged or upside down underneath these challenges. This is where the higher power God - steps in.

Think about taking time for yourself and helping others because it builds relationships that can be *treasured*. It may seem difficult to do at this particular time, but it can be soothing as it heals your baffled mind. Your thinking is changing now, so set some goals this week you can *treasure* forever. Can you make a list of simple ways to help yourself and others?

___
___
___
___
___
___
___
___
___
___
___

DAY 26

(NIV) Galatians 5: 5 **For through the Spirit we eagerly await by faith the righteousness for which we hope.**

This is a continuation from yesterday. Salvation in itself is seen as a gift of righteousness - it is the gift of right standing with God, without any fear or feeling of unworthiness. Note that the way we eagerly wait for that righteousness or right standing is by faith! Faith means to believe in that higher power (you remember?)

We eagerly wait... We should not lose hope because faith is the substance of things hoped for, the evidence of things not seen (see Heb 11:1)

Keep a list of acts of kindness shown to you this week, and show some sort of gratitude, either by calls, cards, text or email.

DAY 27

(BBE) Hebrews 11:1 **Now faith is the substance of things hoped for, and the sign that the things not seen are true.**

A good place to pick up from yesterday, right? Definitely! So, the substance of things hoped for and the sign that things not seen are true will be found in how we eagerly await that higher power - God's power- by faith in the time of need!

Hebrews 11 went ahead to tell us accounts of people who eagerly awaited God's righteousness by faith. Hebrews 11 is a good example for people going through tough times with cancer, and hard times in general.

Inspire someone you appreciate today, to let them know what they are doing is worthy. Perhaps a nurse, therapist, clerk, custodian, teacher, coworker, church member, family, friend etc.

DAY 28

(NIV) 16 **By faith in the name of Jesus, this man whom you see and know was made strong.**

What's faith for? If faith is the substance of things hoped for and the sign that things not seen will surely come…

When Whit first had the stroke, we continued to keep our faith and hope alive. The team of doctors were so amazed at our remarkable strength, they revisited us to make sure that we understood the cancer diagnoses. The cancer had spread throughout all his bones up to his brain. Whit explained to them yes, and then he pointed up signifying that he had already given the circumstance over and put his trust in God. I supported him and thanked God the cancer was not in any of his organs.

I believe when we exercise our faith, even a cancer patient can be made whole by faith in the name of Jesus and their families can be made whole by the same faith. A cancer diagnosis is not a death wish. Faith teaches us that this world is not our eternal home.

Motivate and encourage someone who may be having a bad day, week or is in a bad situation.

Introducing
Days 29-35
Joy
Game Changer
Sexual Healing And Sex Therapy

DAY 29

(ESV) Psalm 119: 48 **I will lift up my hands toward your commandments, which I love, and I will meditate on your statutes.**

How do we build faith? You can't build faith by listening to words that bring fear and doubt. This can come as evil thoughts - evil thinking is simply expecting evil to happen instead of good and it can also come from our close relatives, friends or even one's spouse. Remember Job, he entertained evil thoughts (that something bad could happen to his kids) and it did happen, then the next words of doubt came from his wife! Stay with God's word and build your faith!

In many cases, when men get prostate cancer intimacy in the marriage suffers. I refused to be like Job's wife. Our marriage was based on more than great sex. We learned to be good listeners and communicators and could teach each other our needs and wants. We both had been in previous failed marriages and learned the importance of communication which helped us to become best friends and confidants to each other. Of course, prostate cancer may have hindered some intimate moments, but unlike Job's wife, we did not allow those moments to steal all of joy.

What *hidden* thoughts come to mind from reading and digging deeper into the scriptures, and what can you *treasure* and be thankful for from them?

DAY 30

(KJV) Isaiah 54: 17 **No weapon that is formed against thee shall prosper;**

One of the weapons the enemy uses against you is planting seeds of doubt in a person's heart through evil thoughts or from the words of our loved ones. But we must guard against the enemy's weapon. How? Yesterday, we declared that no weapon formed against our intimacy and love would prosper. Our sex life suffered a few discomforts, but God had a plan for that as well. Although we had gotten older, we had new insights on how to rekindle the flames.

We built faith by staying with God's word, and that weapon can raise anything that is dead (If you know what I mean). Imagine a battle, the enemy has a weapon, but you do not have any weapons of your own, that might not end well right? So, the way no weapon formed against us will not prosper is to arm ourselves with our own weapon and that is the word of God! We stood on God's word by faith - no weapon formed against us will ever prosper - keep that on your lips (If you know what I mean)!

How has God helped you, a *broken vessel*, cope with your current situation and improve your days?

DAY 31

(KJV) Psalm 139:14 **I will praise thee; for I am fearfully and wonderfully made:**

Whit never looked like what he was going through. It was not until a few months prior to his death, he started to use a cane and others knew something was different with him. In our beginning years, women considered him *eye-candy* (handsome). Whit and I believed in having a good time. Whit was not an alcoholic, but he sure could drink some liquor especially Schlitz Malt Liquor Bull and listen to the blues. But even then, he had a certain charisma and walk that set him apart from others. Others knew he was fearfully and wonderfully made.

As years continued, Whit drew closer to God bringing with him many of the friends he enjoyed when he had a good time. Whit drew closer to God by developing a relationship with him. Because the scripture teaches us that all things work together for the good of those who love God, nothing is ever wasted. God used Whit's experiences good and bad to save him and others.

Is there anything else, or another *broken* area in your life, or something or someone dear to you, that you need God to move in, fix or make better?

_____
_____
_____
_____
_____
_____
_____
_____
_____
_____
_____
_____
_____
_____
_____

DAY 32

(KJV) Mark16:15 **And he said unto them, Go ye into all the world, and preach the gospel to every creature.**

I started journaling more through Whit's sickness. In 2008, he was diagnosed with Prostate Cancer, and in 2016 he was diagnosed with cancer in the eye –lymphoma. As I started to post on social media my journey through it all, people began to respond and said that it was helping so many people. Several people informed me that they were going through similar situations and would like to share their stories. With that, I hoped to create a devotion allowing people to journal and be expressive of their journey. This was my way of going into all the world sharing the good news and the favor God had shown to us during our journey.

Think about taking time for yourself and helping others because it builds relationships that can be *treasured*. It may seem difficult to do at this particular time, but it can be soothing as it heals your baffled mind. Your thinking is changing now, so set some goals this week you can *treasure* forever. Can you make a list of simple ways to help yourself and others?

_____
_____
_____
_____
_____
_____
_____
_____
_____
_____
_____
_____

DAY 33

(KJV) Psalm 5:11 **But let all those that put their trust in thee rejoice: let them even shout for joy, because thou defends them: let them also that love thy name be joyful in thee.**

We have seen how trust is important in our relationship with God and the end result of putting our trust in Him. Furthermore, we will see that there is gladness, rejoicing in trusting in God. Things might not always turn out the way we want them to, but things will always turn out the way God wants them to. For example, Whit and I did not always have a perfect marriage because were not perfect people; however, the same trust we placed in God to sustain our Christian marriage was the same trust we placed in God to overcome cancer rather it be through physical healing of the body or Whit being absent from the body, meaning he is present with the Lord.

We will therefore shout for joy in spite and despite because God is our defense in all situations.

Keep a list of acts of kindness shown to you this week, and show some sort of gratitude, either by calls, cards, text or email.

_____
_____
_____
_____
_____
_____
_____
_____
_____
_____
_____
_____
_____
_____
_____
_____
_____
_____
_____
_____
_____
_____

DAY 34

(KJV) Ecclesiastes 2:26 **For God giveth to a man that is good in His sight wisdom, and knowledge, and joy:**

Whit was a Senior Nuclear Security Officer, and his position afforded him the opportunity to train many of his coworkers. While training his colleagues, Whit shared many of his own insights about his personal experiences helping several others with the privacy of their prostate concerns. My husband was a wise man. He used time allotted to train them to plant seeds of Christianity. He encouraged people to stay in their marriages, stay on the job, and to serve their country. He enjoyed mentoring them. He was a man who loved the Lord. A day prior to Whit's transitioning, Whit stated he was ready to go home.

A couple of hours prior to his passing, the social worker came, and documents were completed. This was in the nick of time. God prepared everything for Whit's transition. An hour after his death, the staff gave him an honorable removal from the room and a flag draped box. Even veterans asked how we got that. It was not of my doing. It was just God. He had only served eight years. God placed the right people in his life at the right time. God gave back to Whit as Whit had so unconsciously given to others.

Inspire someone you appreciate today, to let them know what they are doing is worthy. Perhaps a nurse, therapist, clerk, custodian, teacher, coworker, church member, family, friend and etc.

DAY 35

(KJV) Ecclesiastes 3:1 **To everything there is a season, and a time to every purpose under the heaven:**

Whit was diagnosed in 2008 with Prostate cancer and then 8 years later, he was diagnosed with lymphoma cancer in the eye.

May 27, 2017, Whit had a stroke. The neurologist said something more is going on. After days of running test, the neurologist informed us that the Prostate cancer returned.

11 months of fighting cancer and a terrible fall, Whit finally said he was ready to go home- a day before he transitioned. That is just like Whit, a true marine, he transitioned so peacefully the next day at 7:03 pm.

There is a time for everything, Whit's life, struggles and death was at their own time and seasons and God placed the right people in his life at the right time.

I learned and built strength through such times and difficult seasons. We can all take advantage of times and seasons in our lives and use them to build our strength.

Motivate and encourage someone who may be having a bad day, week or is in a bad situation.

Introducing
Days 36-42
Peace
It's A Love Thang
All The Way

DAY 36

(NIV) Philippians 4:11 **For I am not saying this because I am in need, for I have learned to be content whatever the circumstances.**

When Paul said: "I can do all things through Christ that strengthens me," this is what he meant – I have learned to be content whatever the circumstances. I can be content in all these situations, either I have enough, or I am in need. It's not every time we will have enough. It's not every time things will go as planned. But we can find joy in contentment. The journey Whit and I shared was an amazing one. Although we argued, we loved each other and our family deeply. We played with our grandchildren and sought the Lord as one. We had fun with our friends and family. Neither of us shared regrets because we not only learned to love but also learned to be content. We raised a blended family. You can find joy in the gift of family, no matter how imperfect that family maybe or how dark your situation may seem at the moment. One will constantly complain and can even fall into depression when contentment becomes lacking.

What *hidden* thoughts come to mind from reading and digging deeper into the scriptures, and what can you *treasure* and be thankful for from them?

_____
_____
_____
_____
_____
_____
_____
_____
_____
_____
_____
_____
_____
_____
_____
_____
_____
_____

DAY 37

(KJV) Hebrews 12:2 **Let us run with patience the race that is set before us, Looking unto Jesus the author and finisher of our faith;**

Life's journey is like a race. Our walk with God is like a race. There are rules guiding every race, you cannot veer off the track, you cannot run in the opposite direction or any other direction. There's a way to run 'the race'. So, how do we run this race? "…Looking unto Jesus the author and finisher of our faith." Thank God, Whit and I discovered patience early on in our marriage which prevented us from forfeiting our race when arguments occurred. We were patient with each other, and kept our attention focused on reaching the end. We looked unto Jesus and we kept looking at him. This is what the word 'looking' means, it is a continuous tense. There is no time we will not need to look unto him. He is the beginning of what we call faith and he perfects our faith.

No matter how long you are holding out or how hard the circumstances may appear, stay in the race. Ecclesiastes 9:11 reminds us that the race is not given to swift or the strong, but to those who endure to the end.

How has God helped you, a *broken vessel*, cope with your current situation and improve your days?

DAY 38

(KJV) 2 Corinthians 4:17 **For our light affliction, which is but for a moment, worketh for us a far more exceeding and eternal weight of glory; 18 While we look not at the things which are seen, but at the things which are not seen: for the things which are seen are temporal; but the things which are not seen are eternal.**

When Hebrews 11 says faith is the substance of things hoped for, the sign that we will have what we have not seen, it is better explain with our scripture for today. Just as I mentioned a few days earlier, Whit and I shared an amazing journey. One reason was because we saw far more than what we specifically had. We looked beyond what was happening on that day or during that time.

You should not just look at what you are seeing today: the hurt, the lack, the bankruptcies, foreclosures, prison, the cancerous growth, etc. But instead you should look at things seen by faith which is eternity!

Is there anything else, or another *broken* area in your life, or something or someone dear to you, that you need God to move in, fix or make better?

___
___
___
___
___
___
___
___
___
___
___
___
___
___
___
___

DAY 39

(KJV) 1 John 4:4 **Ye are of God, little children, and have overcome them: because greater is he that is in you, than he that is in the world.**

In July, (Summer) of 2008 my son committed a crime, and in October (Fall) of 2008 we initially found out Whit had cancer. I know "winter is coming," but how much worst can it get for us? Yet, it was not until March (Spring) of 2009, that seemingly our troubles grew bigger.

It got worst! In March of 2009, our son was found guilty and sentenced to prison, and Whit had his first prostate surgery. I felt helpless as the men in my life were losing their freedom and manhood. Throughout all circumstances, I kept my peace because what looked like it was worsening actually had it's benefits. They both had second chances.

Our son was removed from a society of familiarity to a place to find solitude, and Whit had prostatectomy, the removal of the localized prostate cancer from his body slowing it down for years and preventing the spread to other areas in his body.

We gained strength from these hurtful situations knowing that when we live with the consciousness that he that is in us is greater than he that is in the world! You should never give up and have peace and know that God is with you!

Think about taking time for yourself and helping others because it builds relationships that can be *treasured*. It may seem difficult to do at this particular time, but it can be soothing as it heals your baffled mind. Your thinking is changing now, so set some goals this week you can *treasure* forever. Can you make a list of simple ways to help yourself and others?

___

___

___

___

___

___

___

___

___

___

___

___

DAY 40

(KJV) John 3:3 **Jesus answered and said unto him, Verily, verily I say unto thee, except a man is born again, he cannot see the kingdom of God.**

Be born again.

Jesus told Nicodemus that there's an entry level criteria into the kingdom of God, and he says, 'be born again.' Nicodemus was like 'Do I enter into my mother's womb a second time and be born again?' You know he didn't get it. Although Whit feared God, he now had a stronger dependency on him. My son was given a second chance from the wayward path that he was on. Now was a good time for them to repent and be born again. When you have a certain peace that God is with you then you can see the blessing in the midst of trouble. When my son told me that he was sorry, I was at peace. It's the new birth! The workings of God's Spirit on his heart!

Keep a list of acts of kindness shown to you this week, and show some sort of gratitude, either by calls, cards, text or email.

_____
_____
_____
_____
_____
_____
_____
_____
_____
_____
_____
_____
_____
_____
_____
_____

DAY 41

(BBE) Psalm 21: 6 **For you have made him a blessing for ever: you have given him joy in the light of your face.**

In this world, we will face challenges but the time in which we are surrounded by this seemingly insurmountable situation is like fleeting seconds compared to what God has in store for us. His plan is to make you a blessing forevermore and to have an everlasting joy. Looking at Whit's life, it occurred to me that we may not all live forever, but we can find peace as we make impacts that will last forever in the hearts of those we leave behind.

Inspire someone you appreciate today, to let them know what they are doing is worthy. Perhaps a nurse, therapist, clerk, custodian, teacher, coworker, church member, family, friend and etc.

DAY 42

(KJV) Luke 6:12 **And it came to pass in those days, that he went into a mountain to pray, and continued all night in prayer to God.**

Pray to Him (start each day alone and at night)

God wants you to speak with him at the start of each day, put your plans before Him. And at night as well, look at our scripture, Jesus prayed 'all night' and he did so alone –he went into a mountain (separated himself from distractions) to pray…Pray for your strength and do not allow your loved ones to see your pain. I recall crying alone, praying alone and it was in these private moments God's Spirit not only comforted me but also brought me peace and strength. Find your peace!

I love this line in Charles Stanley's hymnal – Followers of Jesus

"Fight your battle on your knees"

Motivate and encourage someone who may be having a bad day, week or is in a bad situation.

INTRODUCING
DAYS 43-49
COMPASSION
BACK DOWN MEMORY LANE
I CAN'T STOP LOVING HIM

DAY 43

(KJV) Matthew 17:5 **While he yet spake, behold, a bright cloud overshadowed them, and behold a voice out of the cloud, which said, This is my beloved Son, in whom I am well pleased; hear ye him.**

Listen to him – hear ye him!

We are to listen to Jesus. Hear ye him actually infers to give attention to what he will say to you, listen to him. God says we should listen to the Son. How do we listen to the Son? John 1:1-14 says he is the Word; the Word was with God and the Word was God. He speaks to us by his word and he speaks to us by his Spirit in us (see John 14:26).

God has compassion on us and ongoingly gives us chance after chance. Regardless of the wrong we have done in our lives; God is compassionate towards us. His love and compassion never waivers. God gives us chances to get it right. We must surrender to him. It is never too late to surrender to God. He wants to fight our battle. The battles of our lives are for Jesus and not us.

What *hidden* thoughts come to mind from reading and digging deeper into the scriptures, and what can you *treasure* and be thankful for from them?

DAY 44

(KJV) John 3:16 **For God so loved the world, that he gave his only begotten Son, that whosoever believeth in him should not perish, but have everlasting life.**

Believe in him!

We see God's love in the fact that He gave. More intriguing is the fact that "whosoever believes in the Son." Whosoever believes simply means whosoever believes! No matter the person's past sins, once he believes… well, that's all! The Bible says he is saved! He can see the kingdom of God.

This a continuation of Jesus' discussion with Nicodemus about being born again (you remember?) Now Jesus explains the process of being born again as believing. Believing what? God gave his only begotten Son as ransom for our sins!

Now this scripture gives me a certain peace just knowing Whit knew Jesus, and that he understood God gave his only son as a ransom for our sins. Knowing what Whit believed and who he believed in brought a certain peace to me. I am certain that Whit was born again, and that God will show eternal compassion towards him just like God will show eternal compassion towards you and whatever challenges you are facing.

How has God helped you, a *broken vessel*, cope with your current situation and improve your days?

DAY 45

(KJV) John 8:12 **Then spake Jesus again unto them, saying, I am the light of the world, he that followeth me shall not walk in darkness, but shall have the light of life.**

Obey him!

Have you ever had to search for something in the dark? How easy was it? My first time at the hospital with Whit, when he was first admitted he wanted the lights switched off at night, and a nurse helped with that. But in the middle of the night, he wanted something, I however needed the lights on to be able to get it but couldn't find the switch just in time!

When we hear him, believe him but don't obey him it is like walking in the dark. You must turn on the switch and start walking in obedience if you want God to show you compassion!

Is there anything else, or another *broken* area in your life, or something or someone dear to you, that you need God to move in, fix or make better?

_____
_____
_____
_____
_____
_____
_____
_____
_____
_____
_____
_____
_____
_____
_____
_____

DAY 46

(KJV) Mark 12:30 **And thou shalt love the Lord thy God with all thy heart, and with all thy soul, and with all thy mind, and with all thy strength: this is the first commandment.**

Love him!

Moses gave us ten commandments, but Jesus explained the commandments into two simple task. The first of the two is to love the Lord your God with your whole heart and the second of the two is to love others just as much as you love yourself. How do you do that? He says with your whole heart, soul, mind and strength –that is, with your whole being, everything. Once you have accomplished the first task of loving God with your whole heart, it becomes easy to show compassion and love others as you love yourself.

It's like a marriage, Whit loved me, and I loved him. This made it easy for me to show compassion during his illness, and it helped me to show compassion being his wife and caregiver. Because we were compassionate people, I know if the shoe was on the other foot, he would have done the same. If one party loves, it is essential for the other party to reciprocate in love. We respond with the love in which he has loved us, and that's compassion in a nutshell!

Think about taking time for yourself and helping others because it builds relationships that can be *treasured*. It may seem difficult to do at this particular time, but it can be soothing as it heals your baffled mind. Your thinking is changing now, so set some goals this week you can *treasure* forever. Can you make a list of simple ways to help yourself and others?

_____
_____
_____
_____
_____
_____
_____
_____
_____
_____
_____
_____

DAY 47

(KJV) Matthew 28:19 **Go ye therefore, and teach all nations, baptizing them in the name of the Father, and of the Son, and of the Holy Ghost:**

Share him!

You know you cannot love someone, and you do not tell your friends and family about that person. In fact, Jesus said go into all nations! We've got to tell others about God's love for them! The unsaved keeps no secrets when it is time for them to go out and have a good time. But as Christians, we rarely share the good news about Jesus For example, before Whit dedicated his life to Christ, he was involved with the world rather it was his drinks, a fun time or experiences with the world. However, once Whit dedicated his life to God, he became all about his Father's business.

Cancer is just a bully! The Jesus in Whit was stronger! It is with the same passion; we should teach others about Jesus because many have believed lies about their lives. We have got to share God's love! I often feel the need to speak about my journey to others, and the reason being is because I am required as in the scripture to share Jesus with others. We cannot keep the compassion Jesus has showed towards us to ourselves. We must fulfill the great commandment and tell others about Jesus!

Keep a list of acts of kindness shown to you this week, and show some sort of gratitude, either by calls, cards, text or email.

Day 48

(KJV) John 12:26 **If any man serve me, let him follow me; and where I am, there shall also my servant be: if any man serve me, him will my Father honor.**

Serve him!

At some point, I was stressed out, and realized that I needed to make up some of my doctor's appointments. I was occupied at all moments. My time was consumed with taking care of my granddaughter, several meetings at church, and so much to balance out when caring for my loved one.

Finding time to serve God brought a balance to my life. And yet in all and through it all, the sweetest thing is serving God. Just a kind word can be like honey to one in need of a sweetener. Making one's life available for God to use to bless other lives.

Inspire someone you appreciate today, to let them know what they are doing is worthy. Perhaps a nurse, therapist, clerk, custodian, teacher, coworker, church member, family, friend and etc.

_____
_____
_____
_____
_____
_____
_____
_____
_____
_____
_____
_____
_____
_____
_____
_____

DAY 49

(NKJV) **But those who wait on the Lord shall renew their strength; They shall mount up with wings like eagles, They shall run and not be weary, They shall walk and not faint.**

Suffer for him!

The fact that God is compassionate towards us prevents us from fainting because His love constantly provides strength. Regardless if your end result is the way that you imagined, or far from the result you desired, strength is gained from calling on Jesus' name. Once we emerge ourselves in God's love and compassion, we begin to accept his will and outcomes to say, any way you deal with it Lord, I will be satisfied.

This type of understanding not only strengthens our hearts and souls, but also elevates us mentally and spiritually above the circumstances to mount up with wings like an eagle. Lastly, take note an eagle is rare. God's strength will allow you to respond to your circumstance in a rare way. It does not matter if the church folks, family or friends have forgotten you during difficult times. It matters most to wait on the Lord and he will renew your strength.

Motivate and encourage someone who may be having a bad day, week or is in a bad situation.

Introducing
Days 50-52
Grace
He Promised Me
Love And Happiness

Create in me a clean heart, O God; and renew a right spirit within me.

(KJV) Psalm 51:10

DAY 50

(KJV) Philippians 4:19 **But my God shall supply all your need according to his riches in glory by Christ Jesus.**

When taking care of a sick loved one and the sickness persist for a long period of time or it comes and goes, one's finances will almost drain out. I remember the evening before Whit passed when he started to rub my hand and he said, "You are young, and I know you have certain needs but I can't do anything else for you. I want you to find happiness, but don't let him take advantage of you. You will be okay; you will have enough resources to survive from, but if you give it all away, I won't be here to help you." I realized he was talking about death, and that the Lord had indeed supplied all of Whit's needs and through Whit's prayers, God is supplying all of my wants and needs.

Whit's words of wisdom graciously brought me strength which had helped me to cope with his death.

What hidden thoughts come to mind from reading and digging deeper into the scriptures, and what can you treasure and be thankful for from them?

_____
_____
_____
_____
_____
_____
_____
_____
_____
_____
_____
_____
_____
_____
_____
_____
_____

DAY 51

(KJV)James 1: 2 - 4 **My brethren, count it all joy when ye fall into diverse temptations; Knowing this, that the trying of your faith worketh patience. But let patience have its perfect work, that ye may be perfect and entire, wanting nothing.**

James teaches us to count it all joy when we fall into different temptations, challenges, and potholes of life. Because they are all learning curves and these learning curves will birth patience in us. God's grace is sufficient. We learned days ago to do as Paul said and be content no matter the situation. We can allow patience to do a perfect work in our lives, so that we can turn out as God would want us to which is perfect in its entirety, wanting nothing more. I took the Habakkuk 2:2 challenge seriously. The Lord graciously gave me the vision to write this devotional journal and make it plain to help others for an appointed time.

This is very practical. If you are like me, you will need to write down how you will respond in patience when challenges arise. Be sure to write your responses down in the response portion of your devotion, so you will remember certain periods during your life's journey.

How has God helped you, a *broken vessel*, cope with your current situation and improve your days?

DAY 52

(KJV) Job 29:13 **The blessing of him that was ready to perish came upon me: and I caused the widow's heart to sing for joy.**

I believe you now have a note pad, there is strength in writing things down. When you're going through hard times, being able to reflect back on your journal will strengthen you for future trying times. Your thoughts may go unnoticed, if do not document them. You may just need to be reminded later in life. You may not be as strong as you want to be, but you are certainly stronger than you were when we began. Now, you are strong, and you are a pro when it comes to writing.

I love to close with Job's story, he is one man who went through hell but came out alive. He lost everything and was deserted by everyone. But joy is a personal decision and flows from within.

Cancer has probably stolen all from you as well, it is a bully… But you can choose to count it all joy! Joy is a decision you make by yourself!

But thanks be to God that just as David told us in Psalm 51 that God heard my prayers; He created a clean heart and renewed a right spirit in me. It is my hope that because of God's grace and him doing so, that you have been blessed by what I have been able to share with you.

Is there anything else, or another broken area in your life, or something or someone dear to you, that you need God to move in, fix or make better?

_____
_____
_____
_____
_____
_____
_____
_____
_____
_____
_____
_____
_____
_____

Over the past 52 days, you should have grown in Christ which makes you able to share your journey with others.

W.H.I.T.K.I.M. Daily Coping Mechanism:

What & How I Think

Keep Inspiring & Motivating Others

1) What HIDDEN thoughts come to mind from reading and digging deeper into the scriptures, and what can you TREASURE and be thankful for from them?
2) How has God helped you, a BROKEN VESSEL, cope with your current situation and improve your days?
3) Is there anything else, or another BROKEN area in your life, or something or someone dear to you, that you need God to move in, fix or make better?
4) Think about taking time for yourself and helping others because it builds relationships that can be TREASURED. It may seem difficult to do at this time, but it can be soothing as it heals your baffled mind. Your thinking is changing now, so set some goals this week you can TREASURE forever. Can you make a list of simple ways to help yourself and others?
5) Keep a list of acts of kindness shown to you this week, and show some sort of gratitude, either by calls, cards, text or email.
6) Inspire someone you appreciate today, to let them know what they are doing is worthy. Perhaps a nurse, therapist, clerk, custodian, teacher, coworker, church member, family, friend and Etc.

7) Motivate and encourage someone who may be having a bad day, week or is in a bad situation.

SHARE YOUR THOUGHTS:

MEMORIES

Our Wedding February 1994

Vogtle Christmas Party 2016

"Hurry Kim, Time Is Against Us"

Our Wedding February 1994
Time Seemed To Be Against Us Because Our Years Flew By!

Our Wedding February 1994

Whit And I Became One!

The Beginning Of An Amazing Journey!

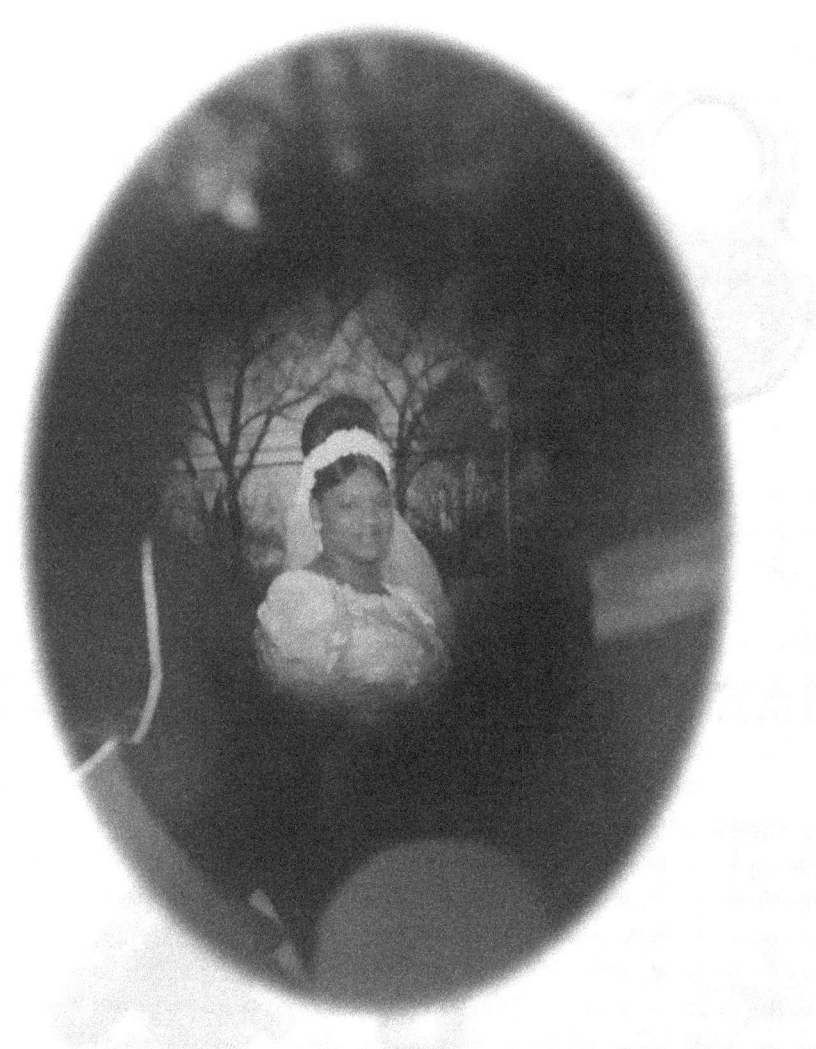

The Beginning Of An Amazing Journey!

Our Beautiful Family!
W.H.I.T. STRONG Treasures

A Beautiful Celebration!

While We Blew A Kiss To You Then,
Now We Blow A Kiss To You In Heaven.

Love Is A Gift From God That Keeps On Giving!

A Few Of Our Second Generation Of Our Treasures!

Our Treasures!

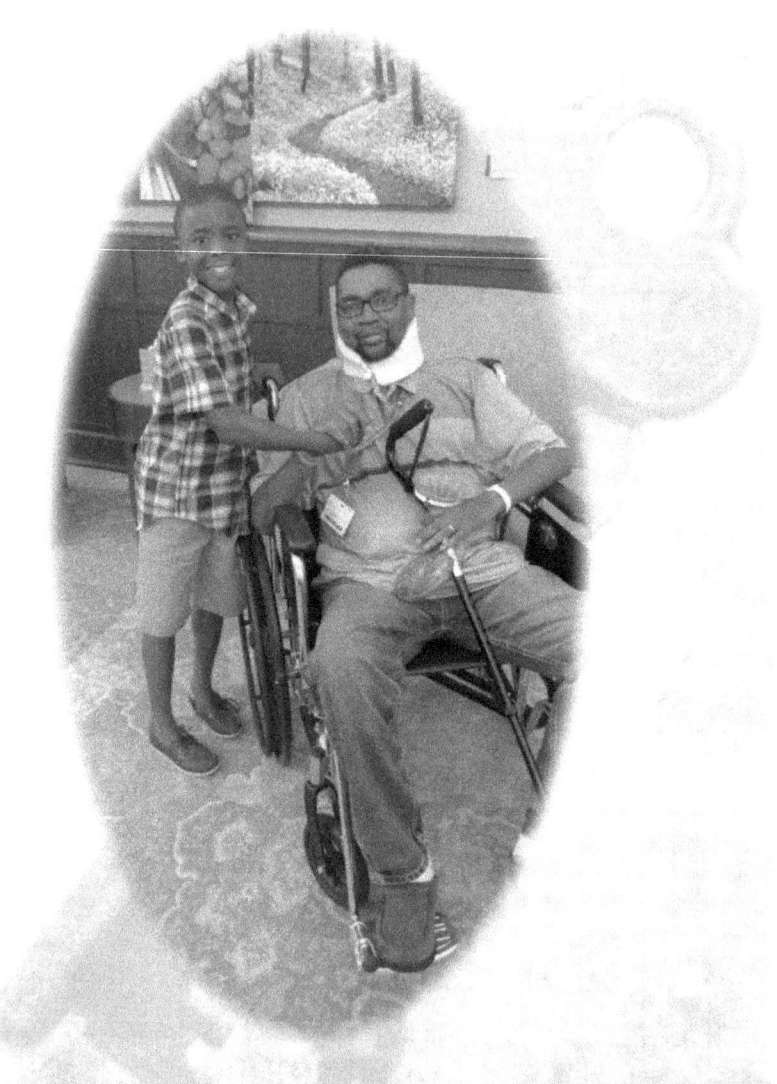

Always Will Be W.H.I.T. STRONG!

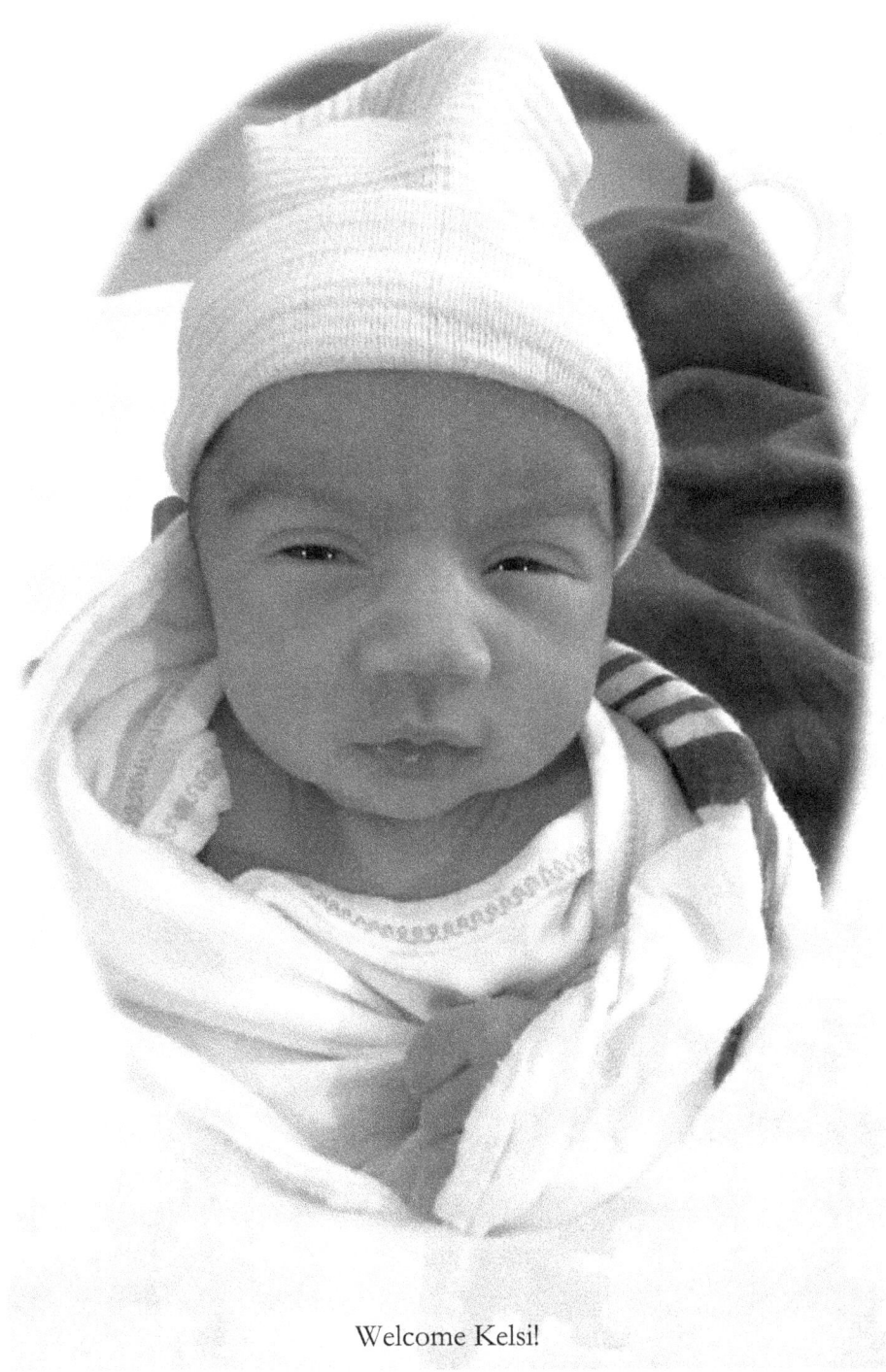

Welcome Kelsi!

Welcome Kelazia!

W.H.I.T. STRONG!

Rest In Peace Granddaddy!

Life Never Stays The Same!

Oh, Happy Day!

Two Of Our Second Generation Of Treasures!

Home Sweet Home; A Door To Love And Peace!

R.I.H. My Love Marion "Whit" Whitfield

God Loves You Best!

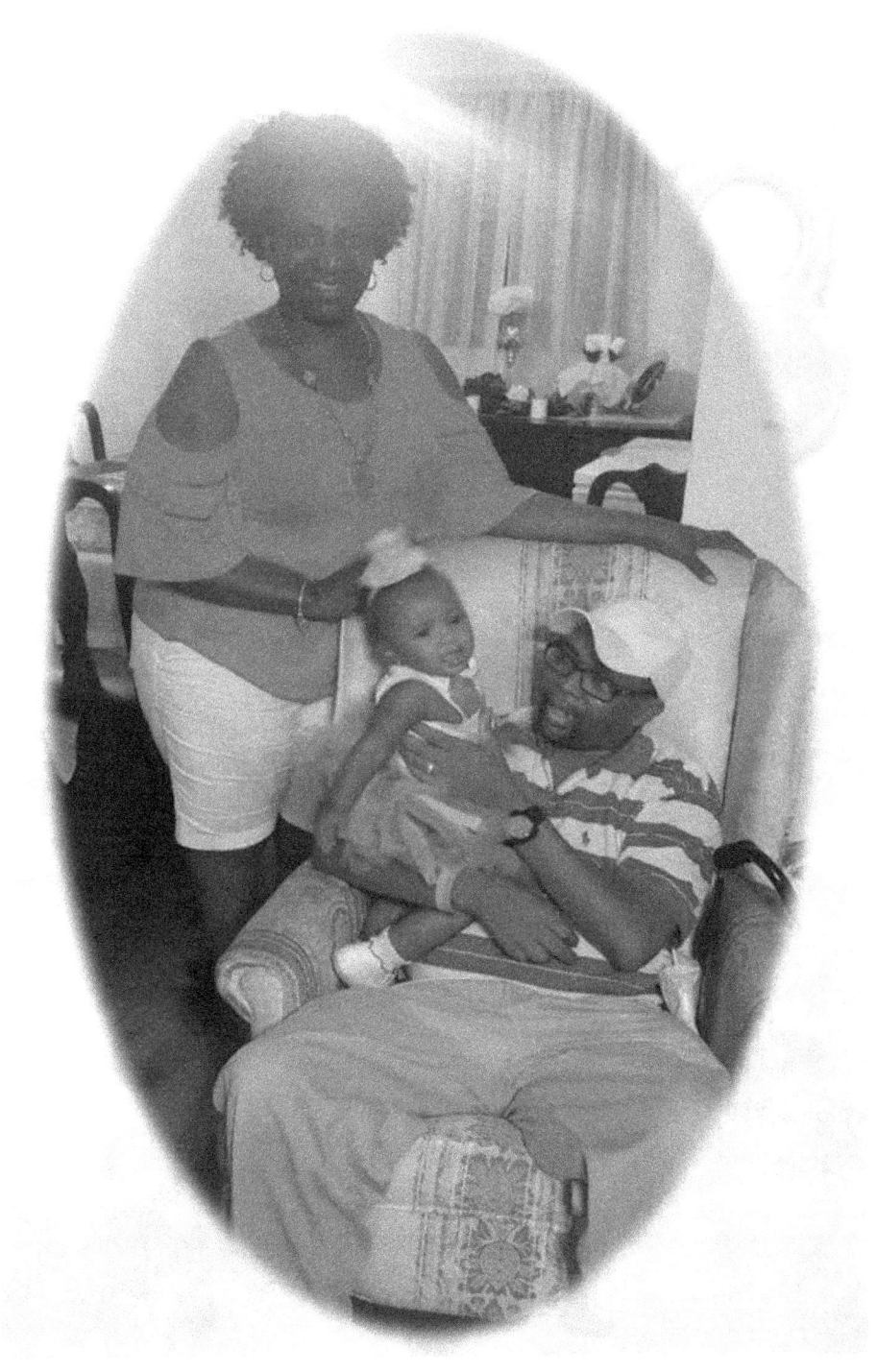

Making The Best Of What God Allows!

We Still Love You And Will Always Love You!

PaPa's Therapy, Little Miss Kynsley!

Cherished Memories!

Whit Loved Serving!

Treasured Memories!

Happy Father's Day!

Where I Came From…

Can Someone Please Find Gwen, Denise And Chris?

A Circle Of Family!

Mommie & Me!

Beautiful Smiles!

Unforgettable Memories!

A Day of Joy Which Will Always Be Treasured!

Treasures From Heaven!

A Day Of Happiness And Of Love!

Pieces of Me

Will Always Be With You.

How You Loved Me

In, Out and Through-

In And Out Of Seasons

Through Time

Without Reason…

Your Love Was Forever Mine!

Happy Father's Day!

Happy Father's Day!

Happy Father's Day!

The Great Miller Fields, My Dad!

Love Is The Chord That Mends Brokenness

And Ties Hope

Around Family!

Forever Mine

Because Your My Kind!

Happy Father's Day!

Conclusion

IN CONCLUSION of me sharing my life's journey…

Those things that came to test, hurt, destroy or even kill me….

Somehow moments of agony

Became victory over defeat

And sometimes we have to choose…

I get it; It's hard to play by the golden rules.

Sometimes it hurts to hush when you want to speak.

Yes, it hurts praying when you are falling apart,

But I always remembered God loved me even if I felt weak.

HE loved me with all of His heart

I hope you take this journal and begin to survive your storm

As I was never on my own, you are never alone!

Kimberly Fields Whitfield

www.ingramcontent.com/pod-product-compliance
Lightning Source LLC
Chambersburg PA
CBHW032119090426
42743CB00007B/399